D1129342

Move Over, Picasso!

A Young Painter's Primer

By Ruth Aukerman

*Dedicated to children who are not able to paint
because of hunger, war or turmoil in their lives.*

Pat Depke Books, New Windsor, Maryland
in association with the National Gallery of Art, Washington, D.C.

Published by Pat Depke Books
Cover and interior design: Jan Gilbert Hurst
Photo credits: T.R. Wailes, Herb Depke, Dr. Karen Carroll, Ruth Aukerman

All masterworks illustrated are from the collections of the National Gallery of Art, Washington, D.C.
Color reproductions of the masterworks courtesy of M.Grumbacher, Inc.

Copyright ©1994 by Ruth Aukerman. All rights reserved. No part of this book may be reproduced in any form or by any electronic or mechanical means, including information storage and retrieval systems, without permission in writing from the publisher, except by a reviewer who may quote brief passages in a review. Inquiries should be addressed to: Pat Depke Books, 1301 Avondale Road, New Windsor, MD 21776. Printed in U.S.A. by Collins Lithographing, Inc., Baltimore, MD.

Acknowledgments

Crucially important for the writing of this book were the help and encouragement of many people and the enthusiasm of hundreds of children in the Carroll County, Maryland school system and in the Young People's Studio of the Maryland Institute, College of Art. I am grateful to all those children, even though the art works of only a few of them could go into this book.

Special thanks goes to Dr. Al Hurwitz, who first challenged me to teach art from great art and to Dr. Karen Carroll, who first helped me to speak and write about such teaching.

The staff of the National Gallery of Art and especially Barbara Moore provided invaluable assistance in research. I also learned much from the docents in their many tours with groups of children I brought to the National Gallery. I am much indebted to Victoria Crenson, Judy Reilly and publisher Herb Depke who contributed so much to the shaping of the book through their suggestions and know-how. For a number of years now my fellow art teachers, my principals and supervisors have given instructive feedback and support for this kind of teaching.

Most of all, I want to thank my writer husband for the hours he spent with me at the computer, and for his loving support throughout this project.

Children whose paintings appear: Chelsea Ankney, Matthew Baile, Jennifer Bassler, Joshua Blistein, Caleb Dean, Randy Dixon, Kevin Eder, David Gault, Ben Groves, Candice Hibberd, Kim Hommerbocker, Matt Hundertmark, Kenny Lowe, Glenda Lozada, Kevin Mastalerz, Casey McNally, Rian Miller, Danny Ohler, Amy Ohler, Louis Pavlovec, Joanna Penn, Brian Raab, Joe Reilly, Jordan Rickets, Katie Rosario, Shannon Scott, Ashleigh Shaughny, Andrew Shorb, Derek Sinnot, Lindsey Sipes, Adam Stultz, Sean Walters, Matthew Watson, Joshua Welsh and T.J. West.

A Note to Parents and Teachers

This book shows how masterworks can be springboards for the surprising and fresh responses of elementary-age children. It focuses on an approach to teaching children that shares with them masterworks of art while leaving room for their own creativity and artistic choices.

Creativity surges when there is a clear starting point, an emotional engagement between child and painting that is expressed in the child's own paintings. Through questions and simple observations, the text allows the child a place to "enter" the scene, discover ever more detail in a painting, to spin his or her own stories and finally to be eager to respond with crayons and paint.

This book offers an opportunity to share favorite masterworks with children. The paintings by other children encourage dialogue, questions and stories and reduce the temptation by young painters to merely copy the masterwork.

The questions and painting instructions are in no way intended to be followed like blueprints. Rather, they are simply suggestions that work for many children and can be modified or expanded.

Become a coach in challenging your children to do their own versions of the subjects, to create their own "masterpieces."

The Painter's Supplies List

*If you are painting with **water-based oil paints* or tempera paints:***

- gray heavy-weight drawing paper, construction paper or cardboard
- brushes of a variety of sizes including detail brush
- sponges and rags
- mixing dishes
- pencil and eraser for sketching
- water for cleanup

*If you are painting with **watercolors:***

- watercolor paper or heavy white paper
- brushes of a variety of sizes including a detail brush
- mixing dishes
- white scrap paper to test colors
- paint board or smooth surface for your paper
- paper towels
- container of water

*If you are using **crayons or oil pastels:***

- construction paper
- pencil and eraser
- soft, wide brush
- watercolors and water
- newspaper

* Water-based oil paints are available from
M. Grumbacher, Inc. individually or in a special Move
Over, Picasso kit. This kit contains the following Max®
Paint nontoxic colors: Red M095II, Prussian Blue M168 I,
Zinc Yellow M249 II, Permanent Green Light M162 II,
Burnt Umber M024 I, Titanium White M212 I.
For nearest supplier call (800) 877-3165.

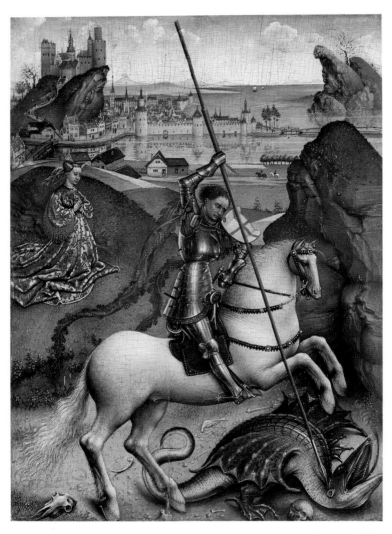

Rogier van der Weyden (Netherlandish, c. 1399/1400 - 1464)
Saint George and the Dragon
c. 1432/1435, oil on panel, 5 5/8" x 4 1/8", Ailsa Mellon Bruce Fund

Saint George and the Dragon

Rogier van der Weyden (c. 1399/1400-1464)

The Painter

Rogier van der Weyden believed that depicting nature in art was a way of celebrating the wonders of God's creation. Although he created a number of large religious paintings for churches, *Saint George and the Dragon* is a very small painting, not much bigger than a postcard. The painting was made for a rich patron who could hold it in his hands during prayer and study its marvelous details.

Look at the layers of scenery receding into space. To see all the detail you might have to use a magnifying glass!

Take a Look

- What moment of the fight against the dragon is shown—the beginning, the middle or the end? How can you tell?

- Do you think the dragon is very dangerous in spite of its size? Why or why not?

- It looks as if Saint George has wings. What are they? Are they very practical in a fight? Why do you think the artist put them in the picture?

- Is the anatomy of the horse fantastic or accurate?

- Why doesn't Saint George hold his shield?

- From which direction does the light come?

- Why do you think the artist painted two contrasting parts in the picture—one full of danger and action and one very peaceful and calm with even the reflection in the water?

Do You Know...

...the wonderful legend of Saint George and the Dragon or can you make up the story just by looking at this picture?

...that the fight between Saint George and the dragon can be taken as a story of the battle between good and evil?

...that dragons are often pictured as combinations of parts of real animals, for example with the wings of a bat, the scales of a fish, the head of a serpent?

Before You Paint...

● Peel the label off a can. Look at the metal underneath and think about the color and surface of armor.

● Look at and touch a toy dinosaur, a fish, or a snake skin. What would dragon skin look and feel like?

● Stand or sit in the position you want your painted knight to take.

Water-based oil

age 10

Collect Materials

● 12" x 18" gray heavy-weight drawing paper or cardboard

● water-based oil paints (or tempera)

● sponges and rags

● brushes of a variety of sizes

● pencil and eraser for sketching

● water with a drop of liquid detergent for clean up

Have Some Fun

● Make your knight a woman.

● Paint a different setting for your dragon.

● Paint a moment of the fight when the dragon seems to be winning.

● Paint a quite different scene of the story, such as a happy ending.

● Do a quantum leap! How would you picture good and evil fighting each other today? How about a battle in space?

Painting Step by Step

Water-based oil   age 9

1. Starting at the top of your paper, carefully paint layer after layer of background landscape—sky, ocean, mountains, hills, rivers, whatever you want. Paint until you reach the foreground of grass or dirt at the bottom of your paper.

2. Again, working from top to bottom, add details such as boats, castles, cities, trees. Remember to paint as tiny as you can in the back and to make things gradually larger as you come forward. To paint really fine lines for detail, use a very small brush and hold it vertically so that only its very tip touches the paper. Add enough water to the paint to make it flow easily.

3. Before painting your knight and dragon, sketch them on a piece of scratch paper. Try again if they are too small or if you are not happy with them. Now think where you would like to place them in your painting. Outline them first with water mixed with a tiny bit of white. Finally place your beautiful princess.

4. When you think you are finished, look at your picture for a day or two. Add more detail where it is somewhat empty—trees, flowers, rocks, bones. Then study your painting again and have someone else look at it with you.

Water-based oil

7   *age 11*   *Water-based oil*   age 11

Red and Yellow Poppies with a Blue Delphinium

Emil Nolde (1867-1956)

The Painter

Emil Nolde was born and raised on a farm in northern Germany. He loved nature and among his favorite subjects were flowers and landscapes. He did not paint them in detail but rather as glowing spots of color and light.

When the Nazis came to power in Germany, Nolde was forbidden to paint. He needed to hide his paintings. Some of them were taken by Nazis and destroyed. That made Nolde sad, but he continued to paint anyway. He painted mostly watercolors at that time because they were easier to hide.

In this painting, which is from that period, the flowers seem almost to weep, yet they continue to glow.

Do You Know...

...that poppies grow beautifully outside but do not keep well in a vase?

...that flowers have petals, pistils and stamens?

...that Nolde strengthened "the glow" of his colors by painting on the back of his paper, too?

...the song "Where Have All the Flowers Gone?"

...how to make colors "bleed"? (Apply them to wet paper or to wet spots on the paper.)

Take a Look

- Of all the flowers in the picture, which do you think is the most important one. Why?

- How is each of the poppies different from the others?

- Do these flowers seem proud and strong or frail and tender? How can you tell?

- Which flower do you think was painted first?

- Why do you think the artist painted the light blue patches behind the flowers? Why didn't he paint all of the background that color?

- There are some "accidental" color spots on the paper. Do you think Nolde should have cleaned them up? Why or why not?

- What in these flowers is not the same as in real flowers?

- Which of these flowers is reaching up to the sun the most?

- If these flowers were people, which would be a child, which a man, which an old lady, etc.?

Emil Nolde (German, 1867-1956)
Red and Yellow Poppies with a Blue Delphinium
c. 1930/1940, watercolor on Japan paper, 10 15/16" x 17 7/8"
Gift of Alexander and Judith W. Laughlin

Oil pastel

age 8

Watercolor   *age 6*

Watercolor   *age 6*

Before You Paint...

- Look at flowers in your yard or garden or even in a flower pot.

- Pick a bouquet of flowers and arrange them in a vase.

- Make a list of all the flowers you know by name.

- Cut out pictures of flowers from seed catalogs or magazines.

Collect Materials

- 9" x 12" or 12" x 18" white paper Watercolor paper is best.

- sponges and rags

- watercolors (or tempera or water-based oil paints)

- mixing dishes

- white scrap paper to test colors

- brushes of various sizes, including detail brushes

- paint board or a smooth surface to paint on

- paper towels for blotting

Water-based oil   *age 11*

Watercolor   *age 6*

Watercolor   *age 6*

Have Some Fun

- Paint your flowers as they would look at night in moonlight. Try painting with tempera paints on black paper for that.

- Paint insects, especially butterflies, visiting your flowers.

- Paint just one large flower.

- Paint a vase or flower pot with your flowers.

- Include the ground your flowers grow in.

- Paint a flowering bush.

Painting Step by Step

1. Stretch your paper: wet it on both sides with a sponge and place it onto a paint board or smooth surface. Be careful that you don't have waves or wrinkles.

2. Mix the color for your first flower, and paint its head (but not yet the stem) while the paper is still slightly wet. The color will "bleed" a little. Next paint the heads of the other flowers. When the heads of your flowers are a little dry, go over them again with the same color to make them glow. Add centers with a different color. You can also blot a color to make it lighter.

3. As you paint your flowers, think of the various kinds and the characteristics which go with them. Paint the flowers in different ways: from the front, sideways, drooping, stretching, etc. Don't use too many colors, but vary each color you do use.

4. Last, using a detail brush, add stems and leaves. If you like, paint a background color like a distant sky around your flowers.

Water-based oil, age 10

age 10

Water-based oil

John Sloan (American, 1871-1951)
The City from Greenwich Village
1922, Canvas, 26 x 33 3/4", Gift of Helen Farr Sloan

The City from Greenwich Village

John Sloan (1871-1951)

The Painter

John Sloan belonged to a group of artists in New York City. They wanted to show that even ordinary life in a city, though not always pretty, is worthy of being painted. Sloan made many drawings and paintings of the city in Philadelphia and New York.

This painting gives the view from the artist's studio in lower Manhattan on a rainy winter evening. It does not show one actual scene that the artist could see from his window, but is an imaginary combination of several different views. Even on a dreary night like this the city has magic and fascination.

Take a Look

- How late at night do you think it is?
- How many kinds and colors of light do you see?
- What kinds of transportation are still running at this time of night?
- Why did the artist paint the streets blurry?
- What kind of creature does the train remind you of?
- Which of the buildings has an unusual shape?
- Why are there no stars in the sky?
- What do you suppose the sign "Moonshine" means? Why is it lit up?
- How can you tell that this city painting was not done in the 1990s? What is missing?

Do You Know...

...what the highest building in New York City is and how many stories it has?

...that in painting you can show more than one side of a building and also its roof? (Think of a block or cube.)

...that many times windows are arranged in rows, and the windows within each row are usually the same size?

...how to paint a blurry effect? (Use your finger or a rag and wipe the edges of the colored area lightly.)

...that crayons strongly applied resist watercolor that is painted over them?

Collect Materials

A

- 12" x 18" yellow or light blue construction paper

- pencil and eraser

- crayons

- black watercolor and a soft wide brush

- newspaper

B

- 15" x 18" purple construction paper

- pencil and eraser

- water-based oil paints or tempera

- water with a drop of liquid detergent

- mixing dishes

- rags

- flat easel brushes of various sizes

Water-based oil   *age 8*

Water-based oil   *age 8*

Before You Paint...

- Take a trip to a city (if you don't already live in one) and look down on it from a high window.

- Use wooden or Lego blocks to build a city. Get out Matchbox cars or toy trains and study them.

- In a darkened room, set a lit flashlight on its end to make it look like a street light.

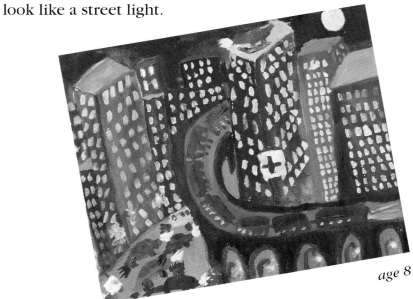

Water-based oil   *age 8*

Have Some Fun

- Show action on one or more of the rooftops.

- Include a building that is lit by floodlights.

- Paint a traffic jam.

- Show the same view but two hundred years ago before cars and trains or a future view with space ships and aliens landing.

Painting Step by Step

A

1. With your pencil, sketch the layout and basic shapes of the buildings, starting with the tallest ones in front. Make some of the tallest ones reach from the bottom to the top of your paper. Work your way upwards with smaller buildings. Lay out roads and a train if you would like to include them.

2. Before you start coloring with your crayons, draw rows of windows at least in the taller buildings. Color the windows first, either dark or lit up. Remember to color very hard and carefully so that the crayon areas can later "fight" the paint.

3. Taking one house at a time, color the walls around the windows. Color things like roads, trains, cars and whatever else is included in your city. You may want to color stars in the sky but not the sky itself. Check that no paper shows through where you have colored.

4. Finally, place your colored city on newspaper and paint a black wash (black paint mixed with a lot of water) over the sky area and anything else that has not been colored. Don't be worried if a little paint gets on your buildings. If you colored hard enough, it won't show.

age 6

Crayon resist

Tempera *age 8*

B

1. With your pencil, do a layout sketch as in A.

2. When starting to paint, do the background sky first, coming about halfway down the paper. Then starting from the top, paint the smallest buildings. Paint downwards one row at a time until all buildings are painted. Let the buildings overlap each other.

3. After the buildings are in, add smaller details such as rows of windows, cars, trains, street lights. Notice the variety of details the young painters have included in their cities. Paint for a while. Rest. Add more details later. Keep working and working until you are satisfied that your city is complete.

Water-based oil

age 9

The Equatorial Jungle

Henri Rousseau (1844-1910)

The Painter

In a poor neighborhood in Paris in 1909, you might have found the artist Henri Rousseau at work in his one-room studio with a bed in the corner. Rousseau never saw a real jungle, but he spent hours studying plants and animals in botanical gardens and zoos.

Back in his small studio, Rousseau made nature fantastic. In this painting, the grasses, flowers and ferns are much bigger than life size and so dense that they almost hide three animals. Even in his largest pictures, every blade of grass is painted very carefully and lovingly.

Do You Know...

...the different parts of a tree? How many can you name?

...that there are jungle-like places in the United States such as rain forests and swamps?

...some of the stories in *The Jungle Book* of Rudyard Kipling?

...how to make different kinds of green? (Add yellow to it or blue, brown or white. You can also add black, but be careful. Use only a tiny bit.)

Take a Look

● Would you be frightened to walk into this jungle? Why or why not?

● How is this jungle different from a forest?

● Can you identify any plant, flower or tree in the painting?

● How many different shapes of leaves do you see?

● What kinds of animals are hiding in the jungle? Did you find the bird?

● How did the artist mix so many different shades of green?

● Why do you think Rousseau painted the three flowers on the left pink when almost everything else is monochromatic (having only tints and shades of one color)?

● If you needed to cut a path through this jungle, where would it go?

Henri Rousseau (French, 1844-1910)
The Equatorial Jungle
1901, oil on canvas, 55 1/4" x 51", Chester Dale Collection

Oil pastel   age 7

Collect Materials

A

- 12" x 18" white paper or light blue or green construction paper
- watercolors: green, yellow, red, blue, turquoise, brown plus white tempera
- sponges and rags
- large, small and very fine detail brushes
- mixing dishes
- paint board or smooth surface

B

- 12" x 18" white or light blue paper
- oil pastels or crayons
- blue and green watercolors for a wash
- large soft brush

Before You Paint...

- Look at and rearrange indoor plants to create a miniature jungle.
- Visit a green house, nursery or botanical garden.
- Like Rousseau, take a trip to a zoo and make sketches of jungle animals you see.
- Sketch your cat (or a neighbor's) in different poses.

Watercolor   age 8

Tempera
age 8

Painting Step by Step

A

1. Wet your paper lightly on both sides and place it onto a paint board or smooth surface. Be careful that you don't have waves or wrinkles.

2. Start painting by applying a light blue watercolor wash to at least the top half of your paper. (You might have to add a little white to get it white enough.) You can use your sponge for this, but don't press too hard or you will get paper fuzzies. Now paint the rest of the paper with a green wash. Let your paper dry.

3. Next mix many different greens. Start painting jungle trees so tall that some of them even reach out of your paper. Each tree should have many of its own distinct type of leaves with light and shadow on them.

4. When these are dry, paint several rows of large plants in the foreground right over the trees. Invent different shapes for them, and again, use many greens.

5. Last, paint ferns, grasses and flowers with your detail brush and hide animals in the jungle. If you like, you might outline some of the plants again. (Never use white or black by itself. Mix every color with green.)

B

1. If you use oil pastel or crayons for this painting, follow the same procedure as in A except apply the wash for the sky and the ground last instead of first. Using crayons or oil pastels gives you the chance to scratch into them with a sharp object such as scissors or nail file. With this technique you can create veins in leaves or fine blades of grass.

Watercolor   *age 8*

Have Some Fun

- Make your jungle less peaceful. Show animals or people in great danger.

- Who said jungles are always green? Paint an all red jungle or an all purple one.

- Add a treehouse or a Tarzan swinging from the vines.

- Instead of a jungle, paint a rain forest or a swamp with alligators and frogs.

Watercolor   *age 8*

19

George Catlin (American, 1796-1872)
The White Cloud, Head Chief of the Iowas
1844/1845, Canvas, 22 7/8" x 28"

The White Cloud, Head Chief of the Iowas

George Catlin (1796-1872)

The Painter

George Catlin spent many years visiting Native American tribes in the West. He was sad to see their native cultures quickly disappearing, so he wanted to record their traditional ways of life on canvas. He spent time observing daily life among various tribes, sketching portraits and scenes of what he saw.

Catlin took around 500 of his paintings and his collection of Native American artifacts on tour.

The White Cloud was probably painted in London, England where the Iowa chief was appearing in Catlin's "Indian Gallery." He wears a necklace of grizzly bear claws, the skin of a white wolf and a headdress of eagle quills.

Take a Look

● What in the picture would make you think this Native American is a chief?

● If a color photograph could have been taken of the chief, would it look nearly the same as the painting? Why or why not?

● From the expression on his face, what sort of person do you think he was?

● Imagine how the chief himself might have felt about this portrait.

● How many different types of feathers do you see?

● What does the green paint on his face remind you of?

● Why do you think the artist painted the background bluish green? Why did he choose not to show more detail in it?

● Can you tell how old the chief might be?

● What ornaments other than his necklace do you see? What are they made of?

Do You Know...

....that the Iowas were a tribe of Native Americans seen first in the area we now call Iowa?

...that complimentary colors such as red and green are opposite each other on the color wheel and, when seen together, make each other more intense?

...how to paint fluffy feathers? (Use a wide, very dry brush with rather dry paint and stipple a second color over a base color. Don't press too hard. Each hair will leave a tiny imprint on the base color.)

Before You Paint...

- Look at real feathers. Touch and feel your own hair or that of a friend.

- Make a necklace of berries or shells.

- Touch your face and feel where your eyes and nose are.

- Dress like a Native American in a traditional style of dress.

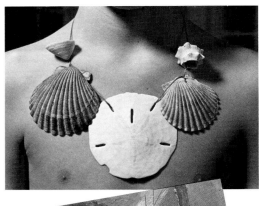

Tempera   *age 9*

Collect Materials

- 12" x 18" gray heavy-weight drawing paper or brown construction paper

- water-based oil paints or tempera

- sponges, rags, paper towels

- flat easel brushes of various sizes

- mixing dishes

- pencil, eraser

age 10

Water-based oil

Oil pastel, age 6

Painting Step by Step

1. Sketch a large oval for the head of a Native American. Fill over half of your paper with it. Add a neck and wide shoulders.

2. Spend time mixing the color you want for painting the chief's skin. Mix plenty. Fill in all of the oval and the neck with it.

3. Wait for this paint to dry before you add facial features. Find the middle of the oval and, using a slightly lighter color, paint the nose. Very close to the top of it, paint the eyes, using three colors. (Think what they are.) You can make the eyes look to the right to the left or straight ahead. Now finish the face by adding mouth, eyebrows and cheeks. Study the chief's expression. Add paint marks to the face if you like.

4. Next paint the hair. Try to mix your own shade for this. When the hair is dry, you may want to add a headdress with feathers or beads in the braids.

5. Now you are ready to paint the base color for the shirt or coat. When this is dry, add decorations, necklaces and other ornaments.

6. Last, choose a color for the background that will make the chief stand out. Carefully paint around the chief. You may need to touch up if you make a mistake.

Water-based oil   *age 8*

Try Something Different

- Show a profile view of a Native American. Have his or her face partially hidden by branches.

- Paint a Native American woman with her baby peeking over her shoulder.

- Paint a Native American medicine man.

Oil pastel

age 9

Peaceable Kingdom

Edward Hicks (1780 - 1849)

The Painter

Edward Hicks was raised by a Quaker family. He was trained in the trades of coachmaking and sign painting. As an adult, he also became widely known as a traveling preacher.

Hicks used his artistic talent to illustrate his beliefs, including his commitment to nonviolence and peace. He painted more than sixty versions of the *Peaceable Kingdom,* inspired by images in a prophecy of Isaiah. The prophecy says that the time will come when all animals will live peacefully together.

Set in a Pennsylvania landscape, most of these pictures include in the background the scene of William Penn making a peace treaty with Native Americans. Hicks is hinting that, in an ideal world, people also should be able to live in harmony.

Do You Know...

...that you can read about the peaceable kingdom in the Bible in Isaiah 11:6-8?

...that throughout history and all over the world people have had hopes and dreams about peace?

...who William Penn was?

...how to show texture such as fur and grass? (Paint a different color in fine strokes over an already colored area.)

...that a landscape painting normally has a foreground, middle ground and background?

Take a Look

● How many different animals can you count in the painting?

● Why are the animals all painted on one side of the picture?

● What time of day and what season do you think it is?

● What is happening on the left side of the painting?

● Who is the main character in the scene on the left? On the right? How are these main characters alike and how are they different?

● Look at what the children wear. How would you dress them to take care of animals?

● Why did the artist paint the big tree and the dark shadowy tree behind the animals, yet kept the left side of the picture in light colors?

● Where do you see texture in the painting and how did the artist make it?

● How is a zoo different from the animal scene in this picture?

Edward Hicks (American, 1780-1849)
Peaceable Kingdom
c. 1834, canvas, 30" x 35 1/2", Gift of Edgar William and Bernice Chrysler Garbisch

Before You Paint...

- Look closely at your dog or cat in different positions. Make some sketches.
- Use your stuffed animals and dolls and arrange them like the figures in Edward Hicks' painting.
- Visit a farm with cows and horses. Visit a zoo.
- Collect some picture postcards of landscapes.

Collect Materials
A

- 15" x 18" gray heavy-weight drawing paper or paper cut from a brown grocery bag
- pencil and eraser for sketching
- water-based oil paints
- flat easel brushes and detail brushes
- rags
- water with a drop of liquid detergent for clean up

B

- 15" x 18" gray heavy-weight drawing paper or paper cut from a brown grocery bag
- pencil and eraser for sketching
- oil pastel, colored pencils or crayons

Water-based oil, age 7

Water-based oil   *age 8*

Water-based oil   *age 10*

Crayon resist   *age 7*

Crayon resist   *age 7*

Try Something Different

● Create a peaceable kingdom for people who do not get along with each other.

● Choose a different season and time of day and dress the children in modern-day clothes.

● Paint the opposite of the peaceable kingdom—animals attacking each other.

● Paint your own dream or vision of peace.

Painting Step by Step

This painting will take quite a long time to do. Plan two or more sessions for it so that you do not get too tired.

A

1. First, you will need to paint the setting or landscape for your peaceable kingdom. Make a layout sketch with your pencil. Do you want to show a mountain, valley, river or lake? Where are they to be placed?

2. Start painting from the back to the front (top to bottom): first the sky, then the pale mountains far away. As you come forward, your mountain ranges can intensify in color.

3. Last, paint the base color for the foreground or platform where the animals are to be placed. When all of the paper is colored, paint details for your landscape: trees, grass, dirt, waves in the water. Show the branches of your trees and give them texture with leaves. You may want to paint clouds in the sky. Only when you are truly happy with the background, begin painting your animals.

4. Look at photographs of lions, bears, etc. and sketch them first on a piece of paper to get them right. Then you can copy your sketches onto the main painting. Paint many different animals, larger and smaller ones. Paint them side by side. Think of their colors and the texture of their fur. Balance the painting by the way you place children or a background scene. If there is still room, paint a mate for the various animals.

B

1. Make a layout sketch for your peaceable kingdom. Start coloring the animals first, working from front to back, larger to smaller. Don't forget to show texture in their fur. Add the children, trees and other details you want to include.

2. Finally, color the background around them—river, hills, mountains and sky. You may choose a watercolor wash for this.

The Tragedy

Pablo Picasso (1881 - 1973)

The Painter

Pablo Picasso started drawing when he was a child. He used many different art styles in various times of his life, showing both happy and painful events.

This picture was painted during his Blue Period, when Picasso's own life as a struggling young artist was often hard and lonely. During these three years, many of his paintings were done in mostly blue tones.

The Tragedy shows three people after something very sad has happened. Could the figures on the barren beach stand for all those who are struggling, lonely and overcome by pain?

Do You Know...

...the difference between tragedy and comedy?

...of a sad moment in your own life?

...that colors can express mood or feeling?

...how to paint monochromatically with basically one color? (You need to mix tints and shades of one color. For tints, add different amounts of white. For shades, add different amounts of black.)

Take a Look

● Why is this painting all blue rather than all red or some other color?

● How many people are in the picture? Who do you think they are? About how old is each one?

● Where are they?

● Do you think they are rich or poor? Why?

● What kind of day is it? From which direction does the dim sunlight come?

● Why is the boy touching the man?

● What is the woman looking at? Does she have something in her arms?

● How is the boy's face different from those of the adults?

● What might make these people happy again?

Pablo Picasso (Spanish, 1881-1973)
The Tragedy
1903, wood, 41 1/2" x 27 1/8"

Before You Paint...

● Cut out magazine pictures that make you feel happy and others that make you feel sad.

● Talk with a family member or friend about what makes you sad.

● Stand like the man, the boy or the woman in the picture. Stand or sit the way you do when you are sad.

● Do something for someone who is sad. Give a hug, share a toy, help someone who is poor or lonely.

Crayon resist   *age 7*

Watercolor, age 8

age 8

Watercolor

Collect Materials

● 12" x 18" white or light blue paper

● watercolors: blue, purple, turquoise, black and white tempera

● sponges, paper towels, rags

● mixing dishes

● pencils

● scrap paper

● painting board or smooth surface

This lesson can also be done with water-based oils or crayons and a watercolor wash. See page 19 (Rousseau) for details.

Try Something Different

● Paint your own tragedy with more than one basic color.

● Paint exactly what could have happened to make the people so sad.

● Paint what these people will do next.

● Still using blue, paint a happy turn of events.

● Paint or draw a sequence of pictures telling a tragic story.

Oil pastel   *age 9*

Water-based oil   *age 11*

Painting Step by Step

1. First, think of what kind of tragedy you want to show and where it takes place. Make a pencil sketch of it on scrap paper.

2. Next, stretch your paper: using a sponge, wet it on both sides and place it onto a paint board or smooth surface. Mix at least three different blues for the colors of background, middle ground and foreground. Paint these washes rather pale so that your figures will stand out well later.

3. Let your paper dry before adding details to the background such as waves, buildings in a street scene, windows and furniture indoors. Again, let this dry.

4. Copying your sketch from the scrap paper, outline your main characters with water only or with a trace of white in the water. Make them important, that is, not too small. Starting with the lightest blue, paint in the color of the faces. Then using different tints and shades, fill in the rest of the outlined forms.

5. Add details last such as eyes, nose and mouth. If you like, outline your figures with a dark shade. (Never use black by itself. Use it sparingly with one of the blues.) If you make a mistake painting, you can use your sponge to wipe it off or you can blot runny paint with a paper towel.

Oil pastel   *age 9*

Oil pastel   *age 9*

Te Pape Nave Nave (Delectable Waters)

Paul Gauguin (1848 - 1903)

The Painter

After he had traveled the world as a sailor, Paul Gauguin settled into an office job in Paris. But when he was 35, he became a full-time artist. In the French countryside, he painted people and their customs within the local landscape.

Later he moved to Tahiti, a tropical island in the South Pacific where he lived for a long time.

Gauguin appreciated the culture of the Tahitian people and painted many pictures of them.

Te Pape Nave Nave means delectable (or pleasing and delicious) waters. In the painting, women and children gather near a little stream. Unlike the vivid landscape around them, they are painted in neutral earth tones.

Do You Know...

...that the Polynesian people of Tahiti loved Gauguin and that he stood up for them and their life style against the French colonial government?

...that color can be used to emphasize something that is more important to the artist than reality?

...that you, like many artists, can depart from using the "true" color of what you see so that you can better express the mood or feeling of a scene?

...the musical *South Pacific*?

Take a Look

● What are the four people in the foreground of this picture doing? Who are they looking at?

● Why is the blue statue of the Tahitian goddess Hina placed in this landscape? How did the artist show that she is not a living human being?

● Find the person in the background who is all wrapped up in clothes and even hooded. What do you think she holds in her hand?

● What is the most dominant color in the picture? Is it true to reality?

● What kinds of animals do you see?

● Looking at the sky, can you tell what time of day it is and what the weather is like?

● How are the trees and bushes behind the figures important for this scene? Why do you think the people are not bathing in the ocean in the background?

Paul Gauguin (French, 1848-1903)
Te Pape Nave Nave (Delectable Waters)
1898, oil on canvas, 29 1/8" x 37 1/2"

Before You Paint...

- Go swimming with some friends or fishing in a little stream.

- Try to sit or stand like each figure in Gauguin's painting. Even stand like the statue.

- Watch the sun go down until it has disappeared for at least ten minutes and see how the colors in the sky change.

Crayon resist

age 7

Crayon resist, age 7

Watercolor   *age 8*

Tempera   *age 9*

Have Some Fun

- Paint Native Americans rather than Polynesians. Add dugout canoes, campfires and totems.

- Paint scuba divers or spear fishers.

- Change the scene into a present-day beach party.

- Bury a treasure on your island and paint people hunting for it.

Painting Step by Step

1. With a pencil, do a quick layout sketch of your South Pacific land- and seascape or island. Where is the shore? Do you want to add a volcano, sacred mountain or stream? Where is your horizon line? Where do you want to place your trees?

2. When painting, never use pure tempera. In your mixing dishes, mix enough of the color you want to cover the area you intend to paint. Don't use the tempera too heavily or it will crack when it dries. Paint from the top of your picture downward, background to foreground.

3. Invent some "mood colors" different from what you would see in nature. Let your background dry before you add trees, animals and people. Mix a rich Polynesian skin color for the human figures. Don't paint them too small. You can show some in action and others at rest.

4. Add hair and facial features only after the skin color is dry. Dress your figures colorfully if you like. You also may want to add details such as moss, flowers, blankets or simple tools.

Collect Materials

- 12" x 18" brown or purple construction paper or gray heavy-weight drawing paper
- water-based oil paints or tempera paints or chalks
- pencil, eraser
- sponges and rags
- brushes of various sizes
- mixing dishes

    This picture can also be done using crayon resist. Apply a watercolor wash over crayon figures.

Watercolor

age 9

Tempera   *age 10*

Le Château Noir

Paul Cézanne (1839 - 1906)

The Painter

Paul Cézanne grew up in the south of France, not far from this abandoned house. As an artist, he often returned to areas like this, where he had walked and played as a child. He painted them many times.

It was hard to pull his easel, paints and canvas the long distance to the château every day. So Cézannne rented a room there for storing his painting tools. He even wanted to buy the chateau, but his offer was turned down.

Cézanne liked to compose his landscapes with little patches of color, which he built up like blocks. Carefully applying strokes and dashes of paint, he seems to capture the feeling of the great house set deep in the woods.

Do You Know...

...that the Château Noir (or Black House) was never finished, but people used it part of the year anyway?

...why unfinished houses feel scary? Think about the story of Sleeping Beauty and her castle overgrown with thorns.

...that many abandoned places have their own legends and histories? The Château Noir was rumored to have been started by either a coal merchant or by a chemical engineer who dealt with the devil.

...that you can apply patches of color heavily or quite lightly, sometimes even letting a little of your paper show through? (Scrape off excess oil pastels with a knife. Use a rag or paper towel to wipe off excess paint.)

Take a Look

- Why do you think this house is called "black" when its color in the picture is orange?

- What time of the day and what season did the artist choose to depict?

- What in this painting is closest to the viewer and what is farthest away? Where exactly is the château?

- Why does Cézanne have so much of the house hidden by trees?

- Some of the color patches or combinations of patches suggest certain geometric shapes. Which ones can you find?

- The windows and door of the house look a little like a face. Do you think that the house has a friendly, inviting look or a hostile, excluding one?

- In composing this picture the artist used verticals, horizontals and diagonals. Which direction is the most important? Why?

- Why do you think Cézanne wanted to buy this house? If it were for sale, would you buy it?

Paul Cézanne (French, 1839-1906)
Le Château Noir
1900/1904, oil on linen canvas, 29" x 38"
Gift of Eugene and Agnes E. Meyer

Water-based oil, age 9

Collect Materials

- 9" x 12" or 12" x 15" gray heavy-weight drawing paper or cardboard or construction paper
- pencil, eraser
- water-based oil paints or oil pastels
- flat brushes of various sizes
- mixing dishes
- water with a drop of liquid detergent for clean up
- rags, paper towel
- knife for scraping oil pastel

Before You Paint...

- Build a house with blocks, Legos or even cardboard milk cartons.
- Look at buildings in your neighborhood that are mostly hidden by trees.
- Look at a book with photos of ruins.
- Build a treehouse.

Water-based oil   *age 8*

Water-based oil   *age 9*

Oil pastel   *age 9*

Have Some Fun

● Paint a house haunted at night or during a thunderstorm.

● Design a twentieth-century home for a president or a movie star.

● Paint a castle surrounded by water.

Oil pastel   *age 9*

Painting Step by Step

1. Draw a simple layout sketch of the building you want to paint. Where do you want to place it on your landscape? Where are the walls, roofs, etc.? Also draw outlines where you may want to paint a road, a river or trees. Do not draw detail such as windows, stones or leaves.

2. Start painting the sky first. If you are using oil pastels, color little patches at a time with different shades of blue, gray, white or other pastel tones. Smear them a little with your finger where they touch one another.

3. Use the same technique when you color in your house. As you paint or color, you can work in your details—doors, windows, gates.

4. Next, work on the foreground. Is it made up of rocks, trees, road, grass, water? Again compose it with patches of different colors. Last, paint or color the trees in the foreground. Make some of them tall enough to reach out of the picture. Show their trunks, branches and twigs before you add color for their leaves. Keep checking your composition for horizontals, verticals and diagonals as well as for color balance and vibrancy.

5. Step back and look at your painting every now and then. Don't overwork this one. Keep it airy.

Crayon resist

age 6

Mother and Child
Gypsy Woman with Baby

The Painters

Mary Cassatt (1844-1926)

Although she was born and raised in America, Mary Cassatt spent her life as an artist in Paris, France. There she concentrated on painting portraits and studies of people. She became very popular through her paintings of mothers and children.

In this painting, Cassatt uses only a few colors, but many different variations of them. Just like the two mirrors, the colors reflect warmth and happiness.

Amedeo Modigliani (1884-1920)

Encouraged by his mother, the Italian artist Modigliani started to paint seriously when he was fourteen years old. Mostly he painted sensitive portraits of people around him, giving them long necks and faces and almond-shaped eyes. Modigliani had a short and very difficult life, but *Gypsy Woman with Baby* was created at a happy time for the artist, shortly after the birth of his only daughter.

Take a Look

- How are the two paintings alike? How are they different?

- Why did the artists choose such different colors?

- Which painting feels more true to life to you? Why?

- How does the Cassatt painting make you feel? How does the Modigliani painting make you feel?

- Look carefully at the clothes, colors, settings and expressions in both paintings. What do they tell you about each mother and child?

- What is each mother looking at?

- Which mother is more like your own? Why?

- Both artists use diagonals (movement between opposite corners) to make their paintings more dynamic. Can you find the diagonals?

- What makes the two children look so different from each other?

- Can you tell what time of year it is in each painting? How?

Mary Cassatt (American, 1844-1926)
Mother and Child
c. 1905, Canvas, 36 1/4" x 29"

Amedeo Modigliani (Italian, 1884-1920)
Gypsy Woman with Baby
1919, Canvas, 45 5/8" x 28 3/4", Chester Dale Collection

Do You Know...

...that Gypsies are a nomadic people who have their own languages? They have often been mistreated, persecuted and killed just because they were Gypsies.

...that Cassatt was very close to her family and visited them in Philadelphia?

...how to make a color vibrate through light and shadow? (Use different tones and variations of a color in the same basic area. For example, color a yellow dress not just one yellow but many different yellows in tiny patches of color.)

Water-based oil   *age 10*

Oil pastel   *age 9*

Oil pastel   *age 9*

Tempera
age 9

Before You Paint...

● Find a photo of yourself as a baby.

● Sitting on a chair, hold a little brother or sister or younger child on your lap. You can also use a doll or teddybear.

● Look in a mirror. Take another little mirror, turn and look again over your shoulder. What do you see?

● Give your mother or father a hug. Ask them to give you a hug.

Collect Materials

● 14" x 18" gray heavy-weight drawing paper

● water-based oil paints or tempera paints

● brushes of various sizes

● sponges, rags

● mixing dishes

This lesson also can be done with oil pastels, following the same steps.

43

Oil pastel   *age 9*

Try Something Different

- Paint a mother and child of a race or culture different from your own. How would they be dressed?

- Paint a father and a child.

- Paint a mother animal and her young.

- Paint a mother and child who are homeless or ill.

Oil pastel   *age 9*

Painting Step by Step

1. Think about where the mother will be sitting, standing or lying in your picture. Will she be on a chair, sofa, a blanket, inside or outside? First, lightly lay out your composition with a pencil. Don't waste time with details such as eyes, nose and mouth. In sketching both mother and child, make sure that your composition is quite large, possibly even reaching beyond your paper.

2. When you start painting, begin with the light areas such as faces and hands. You need to color them completely before adding the features. Next color the hair and clothing. Use patches of color, and if you like, add interesting detail to your dress—flowers, dots, stripes or other designs.

3. After both mother and child are totally painted, decide what your background is to be like. Maybe you want to show a mirror, window, wallpaper, houses in a street or trees in a park.

4. Keep looking at your picture and see where you might need to add more color and detail, whether you should outline your figures or if you want to show more light and shadow.

Tempera, age 8

Water-based oil

age 11